Gilded Cages

Emma K. Smart

Emma Smart

Illustrations by

Sarah Elizabeth

www.sarahelizabethsmart.com

Sarah Elizabeth

TW: emotional, physical and sexual abuse, violence, death, pregnancy-related issues, panic attacks

dedicated to

our former selves
and the healing journey
they must now embark upon

The truth is not the end, it will not save you.

Only you can save yourself, liberating your inner child from the ghosts of your midnight passage, through to the dawn of your healing.

And even after the healing, you will carry the scars,

But ever may they glint in the sunlight as you sprawl across the vast beaches of your growth.

Contents

Moth to a Flame 1

Gilded Cages 2

His Flock of Birds............................... 5

The Truth 7

Noapte Buna, Mi Amor 10

China Doll.. 12

Where the Heart Is............................. 14

In His Eyes... 17

Shades Under the Old Gas Light...... 19

Love - 40... 21

Mother's Warning.............................. 23

Intuition 24

Absolutist... 25

its Due Date 27

Prelapsarian....................................... 28

Sunday Evening 29

for Him... 30

Another Misplaced Dedication......... 35

Her... 36

Love At First GIF............................... 38

How Much Do You Love Me? 40

NB To Future Me 42

The Best Things In Life Are Free 43

He Broke My Heart............................ 46

Hummingbird 48

Nightingale... 49

Ignis.. 50

Just Breathe.. 51

Long Distanced Lover 53

Swagger Unearned 56

The Line 57

The Bad in the Good 59

A Strange Feeling............................... 61

Mournful Remembrance 63

Bigger Than Us................................... 65

Memory of Me.................................... 70

Our Special Tree................................. 71

The Cloud 74

Yin and Yang...................................... 75

Who's A Good Boy?........................... 77

Your Awakening................................. 79

Aurora... 81

A Musical Prostitute 82

A Poetic Prostitute 84

Moth to a Flame

Trailblazing sparks like lightening strike
In a bolt up your brittle arm.
Each hair ignites anew
Caught in rapid blinks.
A blazing swarm, hungry, insatiable.

White searing flame finds your chest
And you are alight.
Bright in your red cloak you hover,
For one golden, infinite moment,
Satiated, finally,

Before the ash that was once you flickers out,
Carried away by a passing wind.

Gilded Cages

Talon by talon they flutter on down
To the gilded cage on Lower Street.
Strutting passed the scratches,
Metallic black stripping gold,
Trampling over feathers abandoned
By that nameless one before.

Who would choose to struggle on such a shining stand,
With this pedestal so high,
Made queen of all this land?

So they sing and dance every hour
To please the Keeper stationed so near.
They hop to the tune of his low melodic hum,
And cry out when he feigns to draw it from them.

But in summer, warm embraces linger overlong.
Could they stretch their legs? Take a short stroll?
No, Keeper won't budge, he's standing his ground,
Afraid to let out what he finally found.

So they peck at the bars, even howl at the moon,

Until Keeper once again hums his sweet tune.

For rinse and repeat, rusting wheels won't abate.

What a tragedy when such adoration begets hate.

Thrust higher than air, suffocating in the void,

Then crashing to Earth, wings singed, heart destroyed.

Now fatigue overwhelms, tempers respite evermore

When the uphill high becomes a burden, a sadistic chore.

They squabble and hiss,

They rage and bat wings.

But Keeper won't budge, he won't do a thing.

Nothing more for it, their forever home assured,

When a feather falls off their mottled yellow coat

And flutters down to the floor.

It settles on the ground, right by the first,

And something catches the eye, glinting among faded furs.

And there they see what keeper refused to show.

Did he suspect, do you think? Did he know?

That under the feather of the one who came before

Was that rusting old key to their gilded cage door.

His Flock of Birds

He sends them swaying with a flick
Of his Cartier wrist
Like the rhythmic caress of grass
In the midsummer breeze.

When he speaks, his hymns
Melt their hearts
Like snowflakes on his palms,
Wrapped up tight in his psalms.

They trust him,
How could they not?
He is the One, they all say so.
And one by one, he tells them the same.

He will save them from sin,
Or did he say through it?
His reverse miracles;
Wine to water-soaked eyes.

So say your prayers, ladies,

Before you go to sleep tonight in his satin sheets.

So focused on your personal prophet

That you didn't notice each other at all.

The Truth

As the lies unwind

And put their feet up for the day

The reaching roots of your truth

Catch hold of me and reel me in.

They twist around my shaking arms,

Then my buckling legs,

Holding taut, tight, tethered

To the dirt from which they sprung.

Each delicate tendril leaves a rocky path

Where it tickles at my skin,

Seizing my limbs with calculated force.

Enough to hold me up,

Too much to just let me fall.

Its branches rip at my cheeks

And vines force their way into my gaping mouth

Until I am choking on them all at once,

Soothed only by a stray

Brushing wordless tears away.

I am laid out flat against its trunk.

There's no bark to my bite anymore,

The anger I felt is sowed into the breeze

That ripples at the leaves sprouting from my palms.

As birdsong clogs my ears

And a thick layer of moss blankets my eyes

I sink into that restless state of perception

That comes when you seek out the truth,

But it finds you.

Noapte Buna, Mi Amor

Something I do makes you laugh
And your dimples become bullets
Piercing through my carefully constructed nonchalance,
Slicing my composure with a thousand pricks
Until it looks like the starry canvas of the crisp night sky.

So when your breathy whisper comes short and quick,
Each syllable rolling off your tongue
Like the gentle pitter patter of intermittent April showers
On your misty attic skylight,
I think to myself, *this must be love's angelic sigh.*

I smile back, no idea what to say,
Your words as foreign to me
As whatever mythical land you came from.
But the moon reflecting in those deep hazel-glazed eyes
Tells me everything I've ever wanted to know.

So *noapte buna, mi amor,*

Ci vediamo domani, j'espère.

I can only pray that something I say

Will one day cross the vast oceans

That lie between us, as we lie together.

China Doll

You sit there; a fragile copy of reality,

A princess on her embellished throne.

You gaze out into the obscured distance,

Unaware of the ever-changing world around you.

Your replicated smile shows an innocent view

Of the foolhardy world.

You never falter from your elastic grin,

From that dreary beauty which you share with so many.

Your silhouette reveals no hidden flaws,

Or evidence of your age.

Quite the contrary, your youth flourishes

In the shadow of your owner's years.

You rest, politely, where you're told,

No sudden movement highlights your existence.

You are merely china, sturdy yet delicate,

Beautiful yet common: a quondam of oxymora.

You sit there; a fragile copy of reality,

Collecting dust on a mantelpiece for eternity.

Where the Heart Is

You smell like a home I haven't stepped in
For too many years.
The furniture all still where I left it,
The weight of its standing leaving deep grooves in the
carpet.

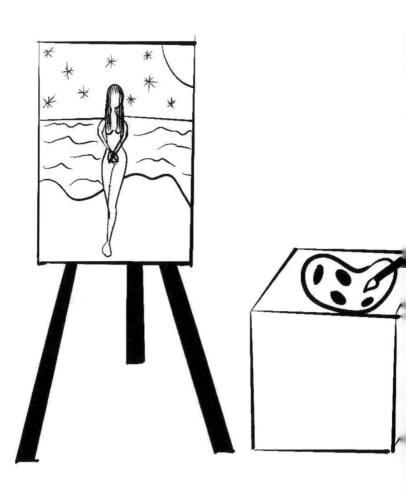

In His Eyes

In his eyes are the answers to the questions

Which incessantly prick the back of my mind.

I see my value mirrored in their glossy gaze,

In that deep yearning which seeps through the haze

Of their delicate dilation.

If I look closely, I can see a woman reflected,

But she is not the figure I critique in the mirror.

This girl glows with a warmth that would put the sun to

      shame.

She could make the earth tilt with the raising of her brow,

She could strip a landscape bare with her featherlight

      caress.

The glisten of her laugh would knock down heaven's best.

Her thoughts are tiny silk petals,

Her words a silent waterfall.

Reflected in his eyes is the mother of all the stars,

The light dancing off her hair as he tucks it behind her ear.

She is safety. She is dainty.

She is the ink with which he will write out his story.
She is the painter who will seize his monochrome palette
And leave his memories infused with vivid golds.

She awakens senses previously undiscovered, dormant.
There is an energy to her, an ebbing and flowing as rich as
        any twilight tide.

I know she is truth because she is sketched
On the most beautiful canvas I have ever laid eyes upon.

Yes, in his eyes is just an imitation,
But what right have I to critique an artist's interpretation?

Shades Under the Old Gas Light

My coat is blue for sure

Like waves off a pleasure cruise, falling softly to ocean floor.

You must be mad, said he

For a coat of ashy grey is all I see.

Well then, my scarf is pink, I think

Like the soft drag of a tired child's blink.

You're out of your wits, said he

For that scarf is blood stained red to me.

Can we concur my gloves are cream faux fur

Like the nestling nudge of a kitten's warm purr?

You're insane, said he

For those gloves are snakeskin green, all can agree.

And what of this bonny orange hat

Like the canyon floor for miles stretches flat?

You're losing your mind, said he

For that hat is as dirt brown as brown can be.

Now I must know madness, my eyes have gone astray,

Slip my grey coat on, I'll soon be on my way.

At last you can see, he chooses to say,

But you must know that coat's blue, definitely not grey.

Love - 40

Match point.
You brace yourself
For the winning shot.

Your tongue a quick whip
Slicing at my forearm serve
With carefully constructed force.

I know before it hits the floor
That I could never catch it
Or volley it back.

Whether it is deserved
Or not
You will win this round.

Perhaps it didn't help my cause

That you sought victory

When all I craved was to remain

At love all.

Mother's Warning

My mother told me what she knew to be true;

It is a dangerous game indeed

Dating those who lack an emotional bag or two.

Of course, you must bear the guilt of being the first

To taint the beat of that heart

By stowing away unto them your worst.

But of the baggage they give you, you must never forget;

It will hurt all the more

For they do not understand the weight of it yet.

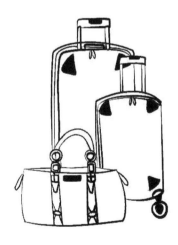

Intuition

Intuition is my oldest friend

And the only one who'll never leave

No matter how long I keep ignoring her.

Like it or not

We are one.

Maybe that is why she feels so alone.

Absolutist

Our relationship is not a democracy.

Those stiff upper lips do not get a vote,

Judging from dust infested chambers.

No, this is a decision for none but two

And an absolute majority is required.

Forgive me then, my dear, for finally playing my veto.

its Due Date

Suffocated. Short sharp breath for premature dreams.

Scream suppressed, shaking pre-rattled ribs.

Crib in the corner by window light overcrowds.

Clouds casting shadows on duck-egg blue, a ghost not yet

here.

Fear in erratic beats of duel hearts, ethereal futures begin to

fall apart.

Prelapsarian

Bald sphere reflects candlelight,

Fingers entwined, slipping with sweat.

The Bell tolls, a cry to the sky.

Feet scream to flee

but the knees are weak; rusty chains.

It is here. It is now.

Judgement raineth upon us.

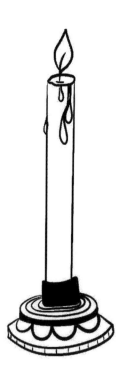

Sunday Evening

This bruise around my eye,

A purple coaster, rest your fist.

Bust lip swells angry, rubescent

At the flick of your finger tip.

Collar bone crushed crystal,

Crescendo conducted by hand.

Break my finger (or four)

See your knuckles, matching set.

29

for Him

Father, please forgive me my sins
For I know I have done wrong.

That morning when flames engulfed
The duffle bag in which she lay.
Icy skin encased in scarlet inferno.

The stench of burning, the reek of death
And she was gone, life blazing, flaring, flickering.
A gasoline haze blurring culpable vision,
Masking vibrant pine and fresh summer dew,
All winged delicacy singed with striking precision.

Father, please forgive me my sins
For I know I have done wrong.

That afternoon when her tea
Developed a mysterious hue.
Toxic service through lethal colouring.

A drop of Sarin, a dribble of Strychnine

And she was mine, hands clawing, grasping, pleading.

She muttered a scream, she chocked on a cry

Until her lips flooded blue

Smirk reflected in glazed eye.

Father, please forgive me my sins

For I know I have done wrong.

That night when blood marked

The carpet, the walls, the door.

Ruby tear stains down a bathroom mirror.

A sharpened knife, a flurry of motion

And she was still, wounds seeping, leaking, smearing.

The monotonous drip of a gory tap

Couldn't dull the image of cold steel

Slicing skin like placing pins in a map.

Father, please forgive me my sins

For though I know I have done wrong

Can't you see that it was your will

That I should my lovers kill?

Another Misplaced Dedication

So another chapter closes,

Lingering between the lines of this barren car park

Somewhere deep inside a January twilight,

Your breath rising as my tears fall.

This time the ink just faded out,

Pressed too lightly on crumpled paper

Until the things worth saying were illegible,

Severing the binding which once held now-frantic eyes.

So I close my book for a time

Until my pen forgets the weight of you.

With well-thumbed faith I await the closing chapter,

But god knows I am tired of turning the page.

Her

I found her dipped in golden honey,

Purring as pulsating light reflected off porcelain skin.

Her eyes caressed mine as we two-stepped

With our hearts, painting music with our lips.

My eyes were closed but I could still see her

And the way the world shifted under her ballerina pumps.

She took the lead and I let her.

My body shadowed hers

Like the dark side of the moon.

I drank her silky whispers

To sooth my bones

And she swallowed my doubts

To quench her thirst.

On tiptoes I ran into her open arms

And we stumbled down a road for two.

Juniper and tonic lingered in our words,

Caramel chapstick on grapefruit gloss,

Chests rising and falling as one

As she span me around and around and around...

Blurry eyes, blinking back light,

The dawn comes swift and sharp.

I reach out quivering palms to find her gone

Our shame and fear left for one

As cotton sheets and blushing cheeks

Fade in memoriam.

Love At First GIF

So your profile says you like dogs,
Well me too, that's a match.
And you like to travel,
Which is crazy, so do I!

Plus you go to the gym,
I can tell from your pics.
I don't but I'd happily try it out for you.
I'm currently browsing sportswear online.

You send me a one-worded response
And I blush.
It's funny, but you always are.
Since I matched with you two days ago
I've been laughing nonstop,
Just hovering by my phone
Waiting for your name to pop up.

One hitch; you don't live near me.

Only here for a week, seeing the sights.

But I guess I could commute,

That's what you do for love, right?

Hey Siri, what does a plane ticket to America cost?

How Much Do You Love Me?

I love you near and I love you far,
I love you more than I love my Pa.
I love you sweet and I love you true,
I love you happy and I love you blue.

I love you weary and I love you strong,
I love you more than I love my Mom.
I loved you once and I'll love you twice,
I love your perfection and I love your vice.

I love you big and I love you small,
I love you more than I love them all.
I love you powerful, I love you weak,
I love your wisdom and I love your cheek.

I love you more than words could say,

Yet my love for you can in no way

Negate the fact I know in my soul

That you're a complete and utter fucking arsehole.

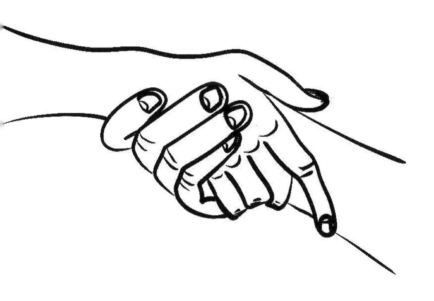

NB To Future Me

The day I start speaking

In absolutes alone

Is the day I should

Stop speaking altogether.

Probably.

The Best Things In Life Are Free

They tell me the best things in life are free

But darling, you cost me nothing less than my mind.

I reminisce you in everything I do.

You're my unescapable, undefined metamorphosis.

If it be true that a fool and his money are soon parted, you

       are my currency.

I was caught in the red.

We withered away into fate's sadistic inevitability

And now what little of me is left is lost in slippery

       distortion.

I can't go back to square one,

All shapes are indistinguishable now.

Nor can I return to the drawing board;

You left your marker pen stamp on it and rendered its

glossy white landscape sterile.

All I do is draw a blank;

A visual stain muffling what you said the day you told

me…

We were just ships passing in the night

And it wasn't until the break of day that I discovered

The excess baggage you stowed away unto me.

With a bay too burdensome, my ship was flipped upside

down

Plunged into blue abyss.

I'm drowned.

You're my opium, and you left me high and dry.

I was swinging for the fences

But the white-picket lifestyle was never your cup of tea,

was it love?

Cloud 9 was our paradise together

Until you pushed me off the edge.

And yet, on the way down my skin tingles where your

delicate hands

Stabbed at my back.

And, with that fixation, I keep forgetting that I'm falling

from grace.

It's raining torn hearts and broken promises tonight, my

dear,

And my cheeks are already wet.

He Broke My Heart

But despite all that I still love him. God knows I

Should hate him but I cannot muster up the strength.

I cannot lose him again.

Give me just one more day in his arms. Or give

Him the power to change. I know I am asking for a lot but

    do this

One small favour for me, Lord. He just needs a little

More time to reflect, a little more to grow. If I don't give

    him a

Chance, I will never know.

true, he broke my heart, but the not knowing would shatter

    my soul

Hummingbird

Hummingbird, hummingbird,
Where are your wings?
Did you clip them, did you cut them
For the nightingale that sings?

Nightingale

In a veil of darkness fly

Over summer soaked storms.

His pitch in perpetual flux,

Too high to let her in,

Too low to set him free.

The night in gales

And tempests will whirl

To the sound of a siren call

And the muffled hum of their curtain fall.

Ignis

Come rest yourself by the fire of my flushed skin

As a swell of sweat sweeps over the beaches of yours

Until molten lust firms, cool and solid, into the stripped

mountains of our union.

Just Breathe

In this way,

Out the other,

In, it screams, back

Out now. Keep rhythm, march

In time, but chest pounds to a beat long

Out of control. Eyes frantic and wild, hunting

In bottomless bearings, pleading, imploring, seeking

Out anything, anyone. My bones are collapsing, caving

In, only empty corridors and vacant parks left to deal with

the fall

Out. Stray shrapnel pierces army lines, breaking down the

aching wall

In between my lungs where crooked branches, tangled and

knotting, pour

Out into swollen veins, strobe pulse, with once tender arms

stained ever more

In starved blood. Saline dripping, the tip tap of a drum,

cries *focus on me*, reaching its hand

Out for asylum, a life raft over stormy pools, to anchor nail-

marked palms, telling me I'm fine, and

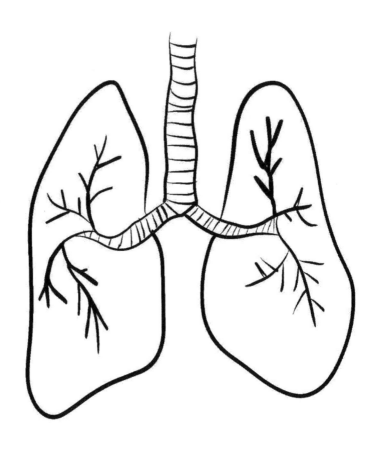

please, oh please, just breathe

Long Distanced Lover

Come-to-bed eyes,
Not a promise but a threat.
Scowl spans space between us
And tips me off my edge.

You leave by air tomorrow.
Suitcase locked, trigger loaded.
Hiatus of the heart, yours quickened
As mine imploded.

Help me believe in love again
Or else that faith will die.
My heart will slowly wither
To tones of anguished cries.

My smile will fold itself away,
Buried neatly in your corner.
My lungs will part with air so sweet
And blacken as they mourn her.

My hair will dull in age old time

As dust begins to settle,

And fingers tremor out of key,

Wrists chained in heavy metal.

Just stay here, my winter sun,

And warm me 'til it's over,

Until I see the springtime lovers

Fly past the edge of Dover.

Swagger Unearned

He walks with a swagger unearned,

Rolled up sleeves, greased hair permed.

He flicks you the Vs, dripping in sleaze,

He is the reason that *prick* was first termed.

The Line

It was just playful, he insists
As his shoulders shrug off
The guilt delicately perched.

I just couldn't help myself, he continues
As the lump in my throat rubs against
Constricting walls,
Walls that were supposed to keep it safe.

It's no big deal, he professes
As the patch of skin he clawed at
Aches under the desperate desire
To rid itself of his touch
And the dirty handprint it left.

Chill out girl, he moans
As though his little game
Was nothing more than a passing note
On the terrible, terrible rain we've just had.

But if it was *nothing, truly nothing,*

Then why does the memory still

Anchor in my gut all these months later?

The Bad in the Good

Nice people don't succeed in life.
Sensitive people don't succeed either.
They are trampled over by those who
Find use in them.

They have no autonomy,
They simply long to please.
To truly thrive you must be ruthless
With a core of steel and bone.

You must be calculated and cold
And disconnected from the burden
Of seeing into others
As though they weren't other.

Perhaps you will be liked,
Admired even, for your kind heart.
But you will never truly be a winner
When the slightest touch will bruise.

The immutable urge to be good

Is a cruel disease

That I would rip out of me, limb from limb,

If I could.

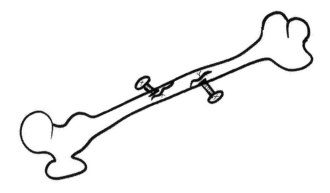

A Strange Feeling

It's a strange feeling

When you've finally convinced yourself

That you're ok.

That this pain won't kill you.

That it wasn't your fault.

That you are a survivor, not a victim.

That you are beautiful and strong and kind.

That you can forgive yourself for the things that they did.

That life will go on.

That there is no bad left to hold onto anymore.

Just good, and the prospect of moving on,

And at the same time

Your heart is still weighed down

Like chains wrapped around a corpse

As it's dragged to watery depths below.

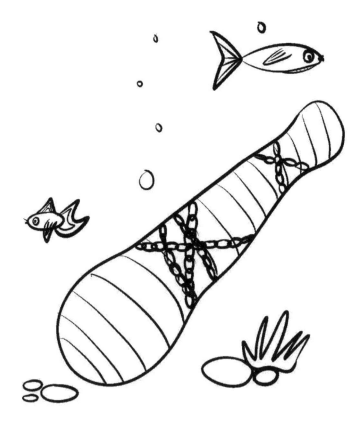

Mournful Remembrance

A wrinkled hand on a granite surface,

Across which her fingers dance;

Sleek, smooth – a miniature monument of mournful

      remembrance.

Marked on this spot her soul will perch,

Exposed to harsh reality.

The words she feared had come too soon, engraved in stone

      for eternity.

Gorges carved into her face by time

Will not disappear;

Neither will the recognition of the departure of her dear.

She clings alone to one lone fact, that

He will be here waiting,

'Til that fated moment when she will, once again,

      meet him.

A nightingale testifies its respect,

Mutes its melodic speech,

As a tear glides gracefully down her over-powdered cheek.

Slowly but surely she creaks to a stand,

And whispers her final goodbye;

"I'll be with you so soon, my love, so whyever should I cry?"

And with that thought she bids adieu.

And stumbles down the lane,

To go on with a quasi-life that will never be the same.

Bigger Than Us

We get so caught up
In the life we've created
For ourselves.

In the work deadlines
And Facebook friend requests,

In the price of petrol
And the knock of home delivery,

In the latest show to binge-watch
And who kissed who at the party.

But sometimes, in night's therapy chair, you are struck
By this moment of blinding clarity.

You're so aware of the world around you
And it truly amazes you.
You are literally starstruck by it all.

You hear the wind trailing like silk through the trees

And it's the most beautiful noise you've ever heard.

You see stars twinkle above you like blinking eyes

And you remember how far away they are.

You know you cannot comprehend it.

You remember that the only reason you look 'up' at the
stars

Is because gravity has planted you in the Earth's soil.

You have been tied to a giant marble with formless rope,

Tossed around in a heartless void for your allotted time.

Just one *snap* and you'd be flung into the impossible depths
of the universe.

You'd be floating off away from all you treasure

For an adventure with a guaranteed end.

But gravity grips onto our ankles and keeps us eternally
grounded.

The gentle call of nature's nocturnal heartbeat

Pulls you back to the moment, and you wonder

What those creatures must think of you in your brick den.

We have self-isolated ourselves from nature.

It is no wonder we all feel so alone.

But perhaps if we just held onto this feeling, embraced our

awe to inspire synergy with the planet that raised us...

Alas, the moment is only ever fleeting.

It has to be for us to not drown in it.

Our phone vibrates or a deadline looms

And we retreat back into our sturdy brick dens.

So afraid of something breaking in

That we forget to ever break out.

So when those moments do come, cherish them,

And for a short while realise that this is our truth.

Or don't. You risk looking like a knob

If you think too deeply about these things.

Memory of Me

Will I be remembered forever

By that stranger on the train

But left behind in the fading rearview

Of those I was once closest to?

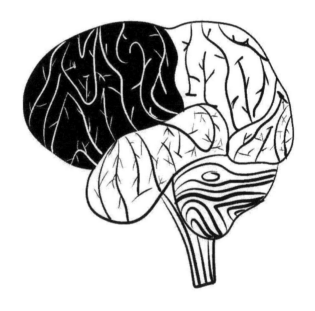

Our Special Tree

On our backs, arms spread,
Staring up at light streaming between
The entwined branches of our special tree,
We traded secrets.

We spoke of troublesome boys, of petty fights,
Of peer gossip highlights.

In the intermittent sunlight our energies convulsed and
        merged,
Our hearts worn on the verge of our rolled up sleeves.

Once a week, every Wednesday,
That hour sketched into our timetables.

Our time, our moment,
No one else was welcome.

That exclusive club, just you and me,
Where membership came with a lifetime guarantee.

Of course, others strolled passed.

Most ignored us, giggling there on the grass.

Some paused for a chat,

Others waved their greetings,

But this was our kingdom.

We dreamed together alone.

Opposites in many ways, the same in others.

My curtains falling carelessly before blinking eyes,

Your curls tangling up with nature's debris.

I miss those summer days,

In that careless haze of our youth.

Much has changed since then, of course.

I reinvented myself in a place far from you,

And I hear you are leaving the country

In which we shared our childhood.

But I vow to you that when I look back

At that time between innocence and yearning,

All I can see are those perfectly wasted hours

Becoming us under our special tree.

The Cloud

What I wouldn't give

to speak to you and

highlight

The difference you

could be making

under all that

limelight.

But it's clear to see

your head is stuck

in the Cloud

Where all your

discarded selfie

outtakes are found.

Yin and Yang

You're the type of person they write books about, not me.

You're Sherlock solving the crime; I'm John stumbling
        behind,

You're the delicious plot, twisting and bending; I'm the
        stale, mundane, predictable ending.

You're the type of person they write poems about, not me.

You're the blossoming rose reborn; I'm the sharp, concealed
        thorn,

You're a profound Shakespeare sonnet; I'm a crude limerick
        graffitied on a filthy car bonnet.

You're the type of person they sing songs about, not me.

You're a ballad bursting with soul, heartfelt and strong; I'm
        the uninspiring lyrics of a manufactured boyband
        song,

You're Mozart, Beethoven, one of the greats; I'm chart-
        topping music's dire straits.

You're the type of person they write articles about, not me.

You're an A-lister with perfect skin, perfect hair; I'm a dirty
wreck downing out-of-date beer,

You're a high-brow activist doing some good; I'm a pesky
youth with a knife and a hood.

You're the type of person they want, not me,

But am I not needed to show how great you can be?

Who's A Good Boy?

Sometimes I see a little of myself in dogs.

We teach them to be good
With treats and affection
All the while punishing their bad behaviour
By withholding such things.

They learn to live for our praise,
Yearning for a pat on the head
To tell them that, yes, they are indeed
A good boy.

I wonder what would happen
If dogs suddenly realised that
They don't need our approval,
That they should love themselves
Fully and wholeheartedly
Without seeking our judgement.

Do you think,

If that day of enlightenment came,

We'd ever be able to

Keep them as pets again?

Your Awakening

Close your eyes, perhaps they'll see

That future, once so certain, eternally with me.

The vision I conjured up of what we could be.

But your eyes are wide, all at once carefree,

Open bright, looking deeper, staring direct into me.

Damnation for us, finally set yourself free.

Aurora

You walk with such purpose through ordeal.

A convoluted strut, two feet grazing the ground

As though there was no hefty paperweight on your plans.

No gravity in your step, only gravitas.

No old black dog whining at your heel.

You glide, a silhouette of the divine.

Ceaseless silence you carry with you

As though nature knows its place is not around you

Because you don't quite fit into it.

You belong in that emerging skyline.

You snap the mould, fragmenting convention.

The crunch of multiple laced shoes on pebbles behind you

Signals the echo of your passing

By others, focused to follow

Your irresistible, commendable, impalpable direction.

A Musical Prostitute

i

People fall in love with the complex.

With the soft of core

But hard of frame.

With the showman's back

Curled away from the cold side of the bed.

II

People fall in love with the contradiction.

With the starlit tears

Muffled in silk cushion.

With the eye's twinkle

At the curtain's close.

iii

People fall in love with the intricacies.

With the quaver thin scar transcribed

Onto that once so slender arm.

With the secrets of the silent lisp

Shrouded in the bellow of song.

IV

People fall in love with the character.

With that laugh, a heart-catching lilt,

That bounces off every soul's corner.

With confident step and salient air,

That eternal *carpe diem*.

v

People fall in love with the vulnerability.

With the whispered doubts

Before the curtain's rise.

With painted skin's shell, allegedly flawless,

That still bleeds when pricked too deep.

A Poetic Prostitute

I split my heart's ink
All over the page,
Words like paperweights
Holding chunks of soul down
As I churn them up.

They're all here.
All the secrets, the wishes,
The dreams and the fears.
The things I want you to see,
And the things even I, as yet, know nothing about.

These playful compositions are both
Fictitious musings for the siren calls of art
And unapologetic reflections of self.

Like a one-sided mirror

This writer is laid out bare for all to inspect.

And so, my friends,

What can you see?

Is it me?

Or the thing you hoped I would be?

Acknowledgements

Firstly, to my lifelong best friend, Sarah Elizabeth Smart, who also happens, conveniently, to be my little sister. Your illustrations brought this poetry collection to life, and I am eternally grateful for your love and support throughout this whole process. You teach me every day how to be a better person, and there is nothing I would not do for you.

Secondly, to my parents, who have sacrificed so much for me (more, I am sure, than I could ever know), all while giving me their unconditional love and support. You have provided me with a start in life that I can never repay you for, but I hope to spend my life working towards it. I love you both dearly.

Thirdly, to Elizabeth Gunning, my rock. You were always at my side, ready to help me heal before I even realised I needed to. I do not know where I would be without your overwhelming loyalty and compassion, but it certainly would be a dimmer place. Thank you for always believing in me, and for being the first to read whatever I put to paper.

Fourthly, to you, dear reader. I delayed the publication of this collection for a long time, through a mixture of fear, uncertainty, and doubt. For you to even pick up this book means the world to me. If these poems have in any way connected with you, then this has all be worth it.

Lastly, to my former unhealed self. It was you who put in the work to heal, not I, and yet I am the one who reaps the benefits of your labour. It seems rather unfair, doesn't it? Be kind to yourself, learn to forgive yourself, and trust in the process. What comes after will, in no uncertain terms, be worth every second.

Printed in Great Britain
by Amazon